How I See the World

There is No Such Thing as a Weed

Jean Frances Callahan

BookLeaf Publishing

India | USA | UK

Made with ❤ on the BookLeaf Publishing Platform
www.bookleafpub.in
www.bookleafpub.com

This book is dedicated to my mom, who, from a young age, nurtured my love for words by making reading a tradition in our home.

Acknowledgements

I would like to thank everyone who has taught a class, planted a garden, or said a prayer. Your hope for tomorrow, a brighter day, and a promising future is truly inspiring. Please know that you make a difference.

I would also like to thank every author who took the time to pen a story, whether in poetry or prose. My first set of books, the *Wonderful World of Disney*, was delivered monthly to a home where reading was always a joyous occasion. Through elementary school, high school, college, and graduate school my mom, teachers and professors always encouraged me to learn and explore the world of words in novels, non-fiction, and poetry. Without their modeling the importance of reading and learning, at any age, I would not have the love of words that I have. My mom has been my constant cheerleader, my best friend, my mentor, and my source of strength. My teachers and professors have taken the time to guide me through the world of content and meaning, the sentiment between the lines.

This book is also dedicated to every person who has crossed my path and given me something to reflect on, especially my fiancé, who has never met a stranger; you are an inspiration. Thank you for sharing your world with me.

Preface

I see the world in words. You and I may look at the same field, along the back-country roads in Vermont, and see a field of wildflowers; some might call them weeds. I see a line of nervous people waiting in the wings of an old cotillion, eager to be chosen. They are blushing and swaying their pink skirts of petal pink, bleached daffodil, and starched white shirts; tittering among themselves, hoping to be brought into the bouquet on the parquet dance floor. This is my world, and I want to share it with you. However...

There is a distinct, unconscious dimming that falls over the eyes of people who do not like poetry. When you mention that you write, there is a glimmer of intrigue and hope, followed by the predictable question: *What do you write?* When I say poetry, it is like telling a new acquaintance you are an accountant; there are no additional questions, and their curiosity quickly dims into a polite smile. Soon, their feet begin to edge away, and you know the conversation has run its projected and predictable course. *I get it.*

I do not tend to read poetry as a daily practice. I have found poems that I like over the years, but it is not a genre that I actively seek out in a library or a bookstore. Nevertheless, when I look around my world, I see it in words. I find myself rhapsodizing about the tightly curled leaves of a new green tree after its winter's slumber in the spring. I see a man sitting outside the coffee shop as a teller of tales, a wizened gentleman who shares the truth as townies scuttle by in hopes of finding a cleaner visage.

I did not choose to be a poet. Poetry chose me, planting a mustard seed that rooted itself and flourished even through the intermittent droughts of joy and hope. Poetry grows and is fed by every nuance of emotion and subtle glimpse of the world I am in. It is the act of seeing instead of looking.

I leave you with this final note: *the ellipses.* That is the name for those three dots favored by writers of old, it means there is more; the story continues, a second thought. And the story does continue. In this work I am sharing my poems and the spark that gave them life. Each entry is accompanied by a brief introduction to what I intended to come across. It is my greatest hope that you turn each page and join me in reconsidering poetry and nudge you into seeing the flowers among the weeds.

A Broken Birdbath

I was coming home one afternoon, and I saw a broken, cracked, cement birdbath in front of someone's house. This beautiful vessel no longer served the purpose it once did, but its presence in the yard, amidst the greater family of feeders, was too valuable to simply discard. The broken birdbath still had a role to play. I had been searching for a way to encapsulate my thoughts and experiences with my grandmother's dementia; but nothing seemed quite right. Then, one day it all became clear in the early evening drive home.

Just after Easter 2024, my grandmother fell in her home, and the discussion about what could and should be done to protect her swirled in our homes and hearts. At 91, Grandma was as healthy as one could be, yet her mind perched on the rim of long ago. Her contemporary memories and conversations were transient and cyclic. Her fodder for conversations often glossy, socially acceptable statements, like the weather or the birds. Grandma, as we knew her, was no longer. The fountain of information she shared dwindled to the distant past, the bottom of the drum of experience and history. Grandma was a broken birdbath. Something stalwart and beautiful, but vacant, except the sediments of memory that lay in the bottom of her mind.

A Broken Birdbath

In the hierarchy of needs, water is a life source.
It is a lifeline to the fragile, hollow-boned, feathered visitors—

A source of life, and a welcomed oasis on a
heat-bleached day.
The birdbath is often the centerpiece, a
chandelier
in a carefully curated garden.

A birdbath is typically composed of cruder
materials,
A composite of gathered raw ore from its
surroundings, craftily hewn
Cement, concrete, sand and stone, the very
essence of earth's elements,
Are the unrefined materials for this particular
piece of functional art.
And, in the eyes of the beholder and
recipient, it is a work to behold.

Its rawness and elemental materials betray its
beauty and longevity.
It holds life, it holds history, it holds a
promise for a new day.
With this precious tenure and responsibility,
a crack in the vessel is life-altering.
It's seeping and weeping of precious water is a
heartbreak for it dependents

The swallow-tailed feathered friends and
curious on-lookers from cloaked windows.

You can witness the crack and view its
metamorphosis
Not with indifference, but a sincere
appreciation of what it still has to offer.

The Life of a Scarlet Tanager

There are moments in our life when we don't recognize the symbolism and weight of a moment, until the rest of the story unfolds. One morning, I was driving to work on the same road I traveled every day, and a bright bird with scarlet plumage caught my eye. I knew the birds in my little bucolic town, and I knew at once this one was a traveler—or perhaps a misplaced soul.

A relative, distant only by the miles between her and her family, was coming home. Home was where she first saw her world and was raised in a family that loved her. Home, on this day, was a place of sanctuary, where she would heal and make choices that would shape the remainder of her life.

The poem that follows is titled "The Life of a Scarlet Tanager." In the world of science, the Scarlet Tanager is an elusive bird. It migrates south in the winter months to South America, but during the warmer months, it travels up the East Coast to live for the summer, somewhere near the Carolinas. Although this bird is bright, it is rarely seen; its song is almost never heard. This morning, in the spring, I saw a Scarlet Tanager, out of place, dislodged from its normal environment, and far from home. It was, in fact, an emissary, guiding a lost child home. This lonely sighting of this elusive bird became a symbol of what would unfold in the upcoming weeks, both in Vermont and North Carolina. It's become a gilded memory of something so bright, so lively, and so rare; a sight I will never again behold.

The Life of a Scarlet Tanager

Exhumed from a state where she never
belonged
She flew to a home that recognized her
Knew her and understood the yearning
To make peace with perceived reality
And what truly was.

Like a tree in the sunset of its life
She died from the inside out
Looking stalwart and strong to outward
viewers
People leaned on her for strength
Not knowing her core had crumbled.

Hollowed out by fear, regret, and heartache
An ache that blocked the sun
From warming her roots, birthing oxygen
She suffocated, crippled by her own
Bad choice or perhaps necessity

Her face etched by time,
Reflected the exquisite burden of living

Depression the color of swampy green
And heartbreaking pale blue
Colored her world, a quilt of experience.

The repeated unfaithful behavior, too
commonplace
To be excused or explained away.
The alchemy of her brain morphed
Into an unknown element
Mercurial, heavy, and poisonous.

Decades of ghosts walking barefoot
In carpeted halls, making no noise
Drawing no attention to their pain
She was an empty vessel with melancholy
awareness.
She would never again be used to sustain.

Something precious and meaningful.
Wearing the face of night,
The sinner and the saint,
The seven syllables of her name
Remained in the minds and on the lips of her
lost flock

The last three syllables falloff, never carved in stone—
A final gift to the living, a final shed of a scarlet plume
Exhumed from the complacent, laid finally to rest.

The Myth of the Watcher

The Myth Of the Watcher is the concept of rumors and the shifting historical perception of a woman on the fringe. I think of Emily Dickson, the reclusive woman in white. I think of Shirley Jackson and her rumored red cape, drawing an abundance of attention to her presence in a small town. I think of Sylvia Plath, who was kind enough to make cookies for her kids when they came home from school. Myths and rumors often twist an innocent observer to an evildoer, someone who harms those around her. The Myth of the Watcher is each of us—whenever we repeat a tale, embellish it with a salacious detail, and allow the story to perpetuate. It is the legacy attached to their name after they are gone.

The Myth of the Watcher

I watch from a high oval window, at the end of the hallway,
One door down is my beloved pink bedroom.
Oh, how I adore the brocade and lace.
Observing with adoration, my mankind, my neighbors by sight.
Without glasses and in miniature, and in the envy old women,
Possess of the young and nimble and unaware and unafraid.
They dally in their commute to work, to school,
To hearth, to home, and to bed, perhaps their own pastel
Tufted duvets with matching en suite.
I watch their dreams tumble, topsy-turvy.

From their downy pillows, shattering unrealized
In iridescent shards, illuminated by a thoughtful moon,
And they never wake up.
I am the watcher, an observer, a lonely, old, wistful woman.

They say she stands on the sills of bare bay windows.
A recluse with a black cat, an old, bony crone,
Openly spying all around.
From above, removed by fear and spying down.
On the philistine mankind, inferior in our simplicity.
To her, we are busy ants,
Scuttling back-and-forth, always in motion with heavy burdens.
They say she sits with the moon.
Keeping watch and taking notes - a history, a diary.
Projecting dreamscapes by casting nets and sowing,
Nightmares that would divide the night.

They say she is the watcher, always watching.

They said she stood in that window, the
rectangle witch's frame.
With the broken pane betwixt reinforcements
and aged patina forms,
Looking down with a savage, pale,
gray-gummed grin,
Having been removed from mankind, she cast
spells
And laughed at us, a smoky cackle with a
throaty disdain.
She was always above us, looking down.
They said she danced on the stars, her sharp
heels chipping meteorites,
Invading the dreams of children
And making them her own.
She rapped on windows with a skeletal hand.
And woke the house, which scolded the dog.
They said she was the watcher, and she never
stopped watching.

At the Pump

Once again, my people-watching tendencies have yielded a poem inspired by the local gas pump. So often, we are known by our place of work, our family, friends, and our enemies. At the gas pump, we are simply consumers, converging at the same time, in the same place, for the same purpose. Our currency does not differ, our goals remain identical. There is a fleeting commonality at the gas pump that isn't often seen in other places. Even the grocery store has the elitist reading label for organic and seeded letters written in script, while others will grab the classic red and white can and move on to white bread with our heads bowed. The gas pump is a great equalizer.

At the pump

We are indiscriminate voyeurs at the local gas pumps,
With slanted, sideways glances
Spying, recording mental observations about each other,
Enjoying our monotonous tasks and judgments all the while,
Standing in the oily patina of our own mistakes.

We scout each other's shoes, assess stitching and badging and creases.
Thrifty, costly, stained and scuffed, off-brand and over-the-top.
The soles betray our occupations, our day jobs, and
How we squander our free time, and our weekend jaunts, and
How we stand when we think no one is looking.

Wardrobes vary, as do care, effort, and intent.
Mothers wear mayhem with aplomb.
Men in exhausted jeans carry insolent winks.
A contemporary courtesy of the young is not wearing pajamas.
All the while, their wives and mothers scowl in acute reproach.

Degrees, accolades, and trophies wield no privilege here.
At the pump, the scholar and saint, the desperado and degenerate
The athlete and the artist are served with equanimity.
Leering until the job is done and our suppositions recede,
The dripping pump is reinstalled as the silent banter is tucked away.
Until another day, when reliance brings us together again.

Silver Belles

Sometimes, a poem starts with a simple, two-word description, and the rest of the poem is designed around that. In this case it was "cashmere jaw"—that downy cheek that older women possess, best revealed in lamplight or sunlight. Fine hair, is a natural part of aging, carries a quiet elegance. Falling in love—that jittery, hand-wringing sensation—begins in our youth and it never quite fades. This poem is for love later in life, a second chance that can only be seized with a second glance. A public marriage proposal,

every bit as enchanting as the verdant,
impassioned proposals of the young.

Silver Belles

He loved her.
It was that simple

He prompted glances from curious passers-by
A flannel scarecrow askew on a bent knee.
With his bashful cheeks and unpracticed
ambition,
His well-wrought hands clasped the expectant
air.
He held his breath.

He was out of place with his gallantry and
chivalry,
A relic standing with a bent back against
nature.
He was brushing up against time—
Languishing, burdened with hope,
He asked her.

Arms akimbo, she mused, both dismayed and enchanted.
She was a perfected woman with a crooked chin.
And a cashmere jaw.
She was incongruous, shy and pleasant and middle-aged,
She was smiling at him.

Within the sanctity of a quiet mind,
She indulged in a myriad of responses,
Tousled around in her mirthful mind.
She chastised herself in the end – there never was a doubt.
The angular jaw bobbed in affirmation as her tears christened their tomorrows.

She loved him,
It was that simple...

A Ballad of a Sparrow

There is a song by the renowned Dolly Parton, "She is a Sparrow When She Flies," I adore this image. Such a common, small, brown and commonly ubiquitous bird in the northeast. The sparrow is nothing of significant importance. But under the right circumstances, when push comes to shove, as the saying goes, even a sparrow can soar like an eagle. Ordinary folk, their feathers hidden in the sweat of the day and the gritty tears of life can ascend like an eagle in the eyes of children. Parents are both sparrows, at times, and eagles.

A Ballad of a Sparrow

He was a broken man with a wing
of downy white and bruised
ragged feathers. The callouses of his hands
remained the only testimony to his drive,
his dedication to being more than the man
who gave him his name.
Those callouses were on the flip side
of blue-veined hands with the thin skin
of the old, the brittle skin of existence.

She was tied together with hand-me-down
threads.
They mended her wings with aged silk,
holding firm
to the bent body contained in the starch of
the apron in
the head of the matriarchal household.
What she said went, there were no hushed
chirps.
Her crooked back bore the weight of bearing
souls,
Raising the prodigies who, in return,

hallowed her name in the familial cry
"mother."

As they twittered and bobbed in their sallow skin,
they bore the marks of the sparrow,
narrow-boned,
fluidless birds without a song to their name.
When the old man and wife - the parents, heard their
title whispered in fear or hope or when seeking comfort,
They spread their tucked, pinched-back wings and soared.
Majestic eagles to every child who bore their name,
They carried the ballad of an eagle and their names were carried on the wind.

Black Birds

It is easy to view crows as a nuisance; they are loud, messy, rude, and they tend to linger in the road too long with their dinner. Since you cannot ignore crows in the Northeast, I recommend studying them; there is a fair amount of research published on the common black bird. They are the most self-possessed bird I know. They are indeed loud and if a bird can have swagger, it's the crow. With a modicum of research, you will learn crows mourn their dead, band together to fend off intruders, and even hold grudges against people; studies show they recognize faces and share the good, the bad, and the ugly of humans with their family.

Black Birds

The roof of the barn, besieged by time,
Had the texture of verdant lush velvet
In the dappled morning dew -
All around, peppering the stillness,
Were a congress of crows holding court -
A cacophony of barks, shrills, a ruckus opera,
Chortles, murmurs, and buoyed chirps,
Telling tall tales entwined
With embellished half-truths—
With ebony feathers that reflect
The azure of a mid-morning sky,
That paints them with broad, heavy strokes -
They are wizened, mirthful raconteurs,
They are boastful boys with boyish grins,
Sliding up to blushing girls
Trying to gain favor -
A pretense to nesting, all-the-while
Demonstrating a gangster's strut or –
A snake-oil salesman's sweep and sway -
When they take flight,
The post-whoosh silence,
becomes buoyed black sails
The flight replaces the prattle of chatter

Of boasts and cackles and murmurs -
They are misunderstood, of course,
Hollow-boned by nature, but possessing
Decorum, a finite set of rules and rituals.
They are seemingly lawless murder -
But they mourn death
With a reverent caw, they solemnly huddle,
Near the lost, a final homage
They are a band of sisters and brothers -
Who take up arms with black beaks,
Defending their homestead in an
Avian aerial skirmish – they dip,
The dive and scold, they remember
Trespasses and trespassers – the humble crow,
A gangster of the bucolic North,
A rabble rouser of the South -
Boastful boys, trumpeting their cause.

Legacy

This poem began as a dedication to mothers and grandmothers, both are groups of women I have trouble capturing in words. I am extremely fortunate to still have both my mother and grandmother; yet when I reflect on their lives, I find phrases that encompass their impact are elusive – how do you distill ninety years of life onto a page? As I continued to draft this, it became a tribute to all matriarchs; every woman who built a legacy through trial and error or simply by existing. Women are often too strong to be confined within the lines of a poem; they refuse to be contained by conventional prose, but poetry may offer a glimpse into the endowment they bestow on their children. A testament to the enduring power of their presence.

Legacy

There are deep roots in the scarlet blood of heritage,

Invisible sinews of tradition and commonality and connection,

Her destiny, path, projection is mine, it is our collective story.

She is my legacy. I am her legacy. I am her storyteller.

She is the fragility of a perfect line of poetry.

Possessing the fine hair that old women hold dear,

Artfully wrapped in a topknot

That turns into a halo in the sun's gaze.

Her memory is a game of hide and seek, angel and mortal,

Angel and mere mortal... time bound.

The fall of feathers, that soundless descent is the noise of tumbled thoughts—

Her considerations of time and place, soundlessly flutter away, no one noticed.

She is a lace maker, this gentle-eyed woman.

Tatting the leftovers of her life into exquisite cloaks that never concealed,

But dismayed the viewer by their beauty... an array

Tightly knotted, with a shuttled loop of
ancient stories, whorls of memory.

The seal may be broken under the right
circumstances.

A length of time that turns even the
leathered remains of harsh lessons and
unforgettable hurt

Into a rotting lace, no longer unforgiving and
hateful and sad, no tethered mind

But somehow, this residence in empty space
becomes beautiful in its decay.

Withering memory of better days, she is
fluent in sacred silence

The idle prayers and the passing thoughts of
old women.

The prayers are the last remaining tenant in
the tattered, tatted mansion of her mind.

She is the legacy, the impact on events and I am her storyteller.

Grace

I love the word "Grace." A single syllable carrying immense weight, layered with meaning. This poem takes the viewpoint of a man seeking Grace; a man who has known ghosts that have robbed him of his peace. His search for Grace is both literal and metaphysical, a pursuit of solace and a person to comfort him; a longing I suppose many of us can relate to. You will read, however, that while Grace often lingers within our reach, our stumbling over the right words, or action, or hearing at the precise moment, can cause a loss, an inability to develop a relationship with Grace.

Grace

The morning was an empty socket.

Where a spectral eye might have dwelled -

In another time, in another place.

He had long-lived in the heavy yoke of sadness.

Melancholy's twin and a sister to the blues.

On this day, he mused,

"I wish to live with fewer ghosts."

He met Grace on a lonely day, on a stoic platform

In a world full of –

"Chances are" and "I wonder when" and
"Perhaps,"

On the outskirts of humble, by and by.

He thought himself a man without
measurable substance,

Trapped in a delicate shell of ordinariness.

Who was he to turn her lovely head?

Hope was artfully tucked that day, in a
dapper pocket

A silken thread of promise that,
henceforward would complement

The golden notions in her hair.

He listened to the wind murmur, mumble and whisper and warble,

The tracks clamored and dinged, while the steam belched and gurgled,

He heard the chime of sincere laugher

Dancing with the husky tones of whimsy – Grace had spoken.

His blandness, his unremarkable anonymity

Did not help him – forthrightness escaped him

And fortitude slinked abashed into a dusky corner of a dry mouth.

He realized Grace and she stared past him

Eclipsing his adoration and dimming his hopes – at first

Then, on a shiny patent toe she turned

She addressed him in cadence with the clinging-clatter of a passing train.

Her words, he imagined, were like a salute –

Bold, authoritative and commanding - he stood at attention.

Fawning and casting daring, furtive glances.

It was a different kind of patient,

One that called on nerves to breathe, heave and sigh.

Grace, uncertain and stunned, but inquisitive,

Donned a kind smile and reached for his anxious hand.

Sweet mentions and declarations of adoring love

Bunched and sucked at the corners of his mute mouth.

Too soon was his abject devotion and time would not stand still.

Grace, caught in the moment, stuttered and stammered in the dizzying sounds

She too was lost in the sliver of unpredictable time.

Train patrons would say he was the color of dry rice – a ghostly rapture,

He felt tipped over, overwrought and precariously balanced on the heels of love.

Until this moment he only existed in this
world

The clack of tracks hummed and whined and
snared the honest ear.

A crooked crowd surged and swayed into
gaping cars.

Grace disengaged and drifted into the motley
of vague faces.

The man felt a void creep into his throat but
inexperience and world-weary fatigue,

Bolstered inaction and silence planted its feet
on his mouth.

In that brittle moment Grace stepped out of
his life.

The View from a University Window

I was at the University of Vermont in the mid-1990s where I attended graduate school to work on a Master's degree in 18th century British Literature and Puritan Rhetoric. If you know Burlington at all, you know that UVM sits atop a substantial hill that leads up from Main Street with Lake Champlain at the bottom. On this particular day, my class was on the third floor of a building at the summit. The windows faced down the hill toward the lake facing west; I could see the sunset in the evening. I am sure we were reading some ancient tomb at the time and the image of a great beast slouching toward Bethlehem lingering in the recesses of my mind.

Too tired to concentrate on the professor's lecture, I found myself staring out the window, watching people traverse the large campus. I arrived at a conclusion. There are two stages of life: the professor, exhausted and world-weary, and the student, also exhausted and world-weary, yet still remembers to smile. The young and the old have so much in common, but there is something lost when the awareness of the world takes over and common courtesy is lost. I'm not typically the one to preach, but I believe a lot could be said to apply a balm or panacea to this world if we would simply lift our heads and smile as a stranger who is as weary as we are.

The View from a University Window

The Golden glow of the campus at dusk
Warms me from the inside out.

Tall, baked-brick buildings both
simultaneously
Reflected and absorbed the fading light,
Sunbathing the black-feathered crows and
Gray pigeons with their ascots of turquoise -
Cooing, making themselves known
On the pockmarked window's ledge.
The mountain becomes pale, muted,
By marked time, it is pastel, an almost
iridescent -
Soon it will disappear altogether.
An old man in dusty shoes and a shaggy
beard,
Remnants of a time once new, fresh, green,
and tender,
Walks with stiff, arthritic knees -
Now unable to genuflect.
He traverses the campus green with its
Kentucky bluegrass -
A broken, tobacco-brown briefcase tucked
under his arm.
His head is low with a cynical grimace,
Marked by the down-turned lips scarcely seen
amidst the beard.

He is tired from the long days and years of
work.
A student mimics the canter in stained,
seen-better-days, sneakers -
With frayed laces and broken heel cups,
He has mastered the loopy, end-of-day walk
too.
Without understanding the common thread
that binds the two together.
His exhaustion is as real in his youth,
As the old man is in his longevity,
But the student remembers to smile out of
respect when passing by.
He on his way to a shared, comically small,
cement cubicle—
A shade of celery green that holds no comfort
or joy for the student.
He manifests himself into his future,
And with loose knees, he walks on.
The professor, climbing into a utilitarian and
unremarkable dark grey car,
Idles slowly down the crested hill of the
university,
Into the golden glow of the setting sun.

The old man is temporarily blinded by the light.
The past slipping just beyond reach.
Then his eyes adjust to dusk, and he accelerates.
He can only see the fading outline of the slow student slouching away,
And the student can only hear the whispered crunch of gravel -
Below his feet as he grows smaller in the rear view mirror.

The Parking Lot

I often describe poetry as the difference between looking and truly seeing. In this instance, it was about hearing and listening. I was in our local, mass market, blue and yellow, bargain superstore parking lot when I overheard two women conversing as they transferred their groceries into their car. One line stood out: "I used to be rich." That was the only factual part of this moment. The rest is a creative exercise in my mind.

The Parking Lot

Her life was a melody with no discernible beginning,
The middle and end lingered in the essence of a few words.
Her face wore a memory like a mask,
And her lips were caressing a lost refrain,
perhaps a prelude to a smile -
A bluesy soundtrack crooning,
"If only...then... perhaps... and maybe..."

I do not know her name.
In fact, I never saw her face,
But an overhead snippet of conversation that resonated -
Caught my attention, and the fragment morphed into a frothy,
"I used to be rich."
It is true, the other side is not far away.

The stage was not clandestine,
No dusky tavern nor a gossipy, garish salon
Where such utterances were common -

It was a parking lot communion, ceremonial
pleasantries.
With pools of oily casting rainbows, and
recording the exchange,
Shoppers passed by, oblivious to the curious
disclosure.

"I used to be rich."
Was it a defense of the current state, a verbal
reckoning –
Perhaps a sense of despair, of a life that was,
That might have been, if and only if the other
side,
Were farther away, and we were not recording
history in a parking lot.

The Secret of Jawbone Lake

This short epic poem was inspired by a name I came across on a map, Sister's Cove. In my mind, such a name would demand another equally unique name; an enigmatic relative town, thus Jawbone Lake came to be. With every mythic, tireworn settlement comes a story of youth spent in nature and the growth into adulthood. So often, we long to return to the shores of our youth; the muddy shores of fantasy and freedom and days spent playing outside without obligation, or reality, or pain or heartache.

This is the story of a young girl, raised on the gentle ebbing waters of Jawbone Lake and returning to the lake as an adult, and a final visit to life-giving waters, for the ultimate time. The heaviness of the language is meant to reflect the power of the water in this lake, in the shape of a Jawbone with its sweeping arc and ragged edges—both protective and perilous.

A final note, in the Bible story of Cain and Abel, there is speculation that the weapon Cain used to kill his brother Abel was a jawbone. Like many towns, the origin story of the town can define its residents.

The Secret of Jawbone Lake

Jawbone Lake was the sobriquet of Long Lake, a simplistic statement of the obvious. The lake, marshy, dank, and dark was a relation to the fashionable Sister's Cove, Over yonder and henceforth named to quiet the bothersome mouth of the fairest sex.

Jawbone Lake was different, a dark-haired
child in a world of pale siblings.
Much like the trinity, the source of the
moniker sprang from three wellsprings;
There was an internal oral tale, an external
nickname, and the progeny of a wild girl.

The earliest rationale was a relic of its era, a
time of stiff-chinned wire-haired dowager.
A woman who touted the scourge that
bloomed from imbibing – a Rechabite, a
teetotaler.
She sermonized to narrow-soled strangers
passing through the sable brown mud banks.
Jawbone Lake was named thus for the jagged,
drunken lines of its shores,
A condemning rumor that whispered the
secret of the ragged cartographer, who
Shared his time with men who possessed
names like Macallan, Baker, and Jim.

The second myth, as stalwart as the sun-baked
brick cornerstone of the church,
Was the epithet birthed in the
swallow-throated vernacular

Of natives whose tongue wagged deliriously with the scarce passersby.
Townsfolk talked and tattled from crooked front porches, bleached whiter than whale bone,
Alongside dusty dogs' tails stirring the otherwise stagnant air–
The jawbone gets its use when an ear and smile is lent, serving as a balm,
To the rusty hinges of a normally pinched face.
Lonesomeness has its own panacea, simple and universal in design.

The final origin lore was the dovetailed reference to the lake's daughter -
For no woman could have birthed such an impish girl.
The name was a token of their rumored fathers, sons of Adam
Whose twisted mossy ire yielded a jawbone to take rank by force.
And thus, the stony, toothy jawbone entered into the annals of spoken history.

The first such bone to shed blood, but not the last to master its whistling arc.
The daughter of a devil, a sinner, a saint, a life force of promise and or fear.

Jawbone Lake cradled secrets on its brocade shores,
Knitted with the gossamer strings of fact and woolen dander of myth.
But the trinity of whispered lore held no veracity – the lake was alive; it was a gift-giver.
The lake breathed. Inhales and exhales could be seen in the impertinent ripples,
Latching to the smooth, time bound witnessed and browbeaten historians
That lined the unkind rocky shores of the saw-tooth lake and its sullen eddies.
The murmuring echo of a mourning dove, singing in the pastel evening – marked time
While the raspy croak of bullfrogs told of the waxing season and the harvest of a fading sun
The lake spoke its own language, never taught, but always understood.

Jawbone Lake was a fountain of sustenance
and a persecuting crucible.
The lake, like its daughter, was a mirror when
the world stood still.
This mirror reflected every gnarled and
majestic trunk, and the knobby knees of the
supplicant
Leaning in for baptisms on summer days; a
mirror that reflected vanity, and heartbreak
and mirth
A reflection of what was, what is, and what
shall never be again, a mirror that reflected
Only that moment and took no heed of the
past nor future. In the water, neither exist.

Jawbone Lake was an echo when the frothy
shores swallowed screams of agony.
Unheralded frustration bound by stinging
pervasive restraint to be seen and not heard
A voiceless daughter whose cloak of silence
was fitted upon her like a thorny crown
Her whispered fervent wishes never crossing
the bridge.
Jawbone Lake is that silent sister in all of us
who seek answers in opaque waters.

We are those who dive into the fathomless
depths, looking for details absent from rocky
shores.
Women born in the straight uncompromising
letters of a doctor's oath,
women delivered into myth by actions, and
witness, and silence and roars.

The daughter of Jawbone Lake learned the
cadence of the lake as a solitary child.
The bare ankles of this godless child sank into
the muddy shoals on a spring day,
When the earth bade the bald low sun of
winter to rise and ascend in an azure sky,
The lake became a bathing tub for a mermaid,
a girl with wild scales of youth and curiosity.
A girl who did not yet carry fear or the
learned shyness of conformity,
She was brazen, wild, and free.

The lake was a bosom confidante who listened
to secrets and held them within a fluid
sacristy

A silent friend who shared the buoyant
braided sweetgrass leis and tiaras of common
flowers
Jawbone Lake was the place where the green
world's daughter found her childhood.
Spring said goodbye to the daughter as the
promises of tomorrow allied itself with
opportunity
And the promise of the hand of a man who
never knew the mythic childhood of the
daughter

That summer of her first adult year when the
bare muddy toes and hard-soled feet of
August
Gives way to the round-toed scuffed shoes of
early winter and the underbelly
Of gorged hawks grows sallow and shrunken
from the dwindling banquet of summer
eves—
The daughter returns to the lake. Seven blue
moons have risen over Jawbone Lake.
She perches familiarly on the shore,
whispering her heavy stories, unloading the
burden of years.

The daughter was no longer the godless
impish child of her youth, she knew the
world.
She knew laughter and joy and hope and
prayers for unfulfilled tomorrows.
The daughter knew tears and terror and the
disappointment that danced with broken
promises.
She knew the sermons of the world and the
gospels of the earth.

It was the Snow Moon that lit the way home
for the misplaced Daughter.
The feeble February light twinned with the
still silvery moonlit water
No longer was it reflecting the bare ankles, of
a secular woman, but reflected
A tripod of twisted, blue-veined feet and the
gnarly time-knotted cane of an old soul.
Bent and broken, the mermaid turned against
her time on land and returned
To the waters that braided her name among
the local lore and the myths of time.

The knotted wooden cane, returned as a promised payment to the earth which received it.

The Old Man

There is a four-way traffic light not far from my workplace; it is one of the few lights I enjoy stopping at. The bustle of people along Main Street, USA, always offers a unique glimpse into a town. While the people are as diverse as their geography across the country, I have seen some indisputable constants. This poem takes a portrait of the elderly in our community. Their posture denotes a lifetime of bearing constant pressure; this is a pressure that often bows their back and slows their once nimble feet to a tell-tale time-honored shuffle. The voyeur, myself in this case, is at once startled by his determination and my own egocentric pity after a long day's work. I sat comfortably in my car with my body that still possesses the ability to skip and gambol and I recognized our similarities and our differences.

The Old Man

The car was warm despite the chill of
October's air.
Worries of the day seeping from my pores - I
felt older than I should.
Staring through the -tinted pane windshield,
I witnessed both kinship and reckoning.

There is anonymity in any town - this man
was a stranger, like the rest.
He wore charcoal and the silver stubble of a
beard.
His gait caught my eye, and I understood;
chagrined for my greedy self-centeredness.

There was a weary but guarded steadfast
exchange.

With the salty pavement as if the hinges of his
knees
We were too rusted to bend with ease, too
tired to speak with their soft-soled soldiers.

The weight of a burden carried too long.
By a hollowed hull of a broken body of the
old.
Nevertheless, the old man traversed a faded
crosswalk, taking time, step by step.

The stale blue-gray exhaust of cars formed an
emperor's new cloak.
It mimicked the robes of an ebbing soul,
Draping the stooped shoulders in a mist that
swayed and rolled with each step.

The soft middle and swollen paunch of the
slouch-shouldered, gentle-man
Who reached the pinnacle of maturity, shook
from
A chortling, wheezing cough - reminiscent of
an old truck thinking of turning over.

We never met, never spoke or shared a vision,
but we shared the commonality of
An unspoken name, anonymity
There are a number of ways to be invisible, I
thought, and drove through an orange light.

Wonder Woman

There is an old cartoon where two kids are standing outside of their mother's closet, holding a Wonder Woman cape and one kid says to the other, "See, I told you." Women are superheroes.

Wonder Woman

She is...
Exceptional.
There's safety in
Being unexceptional,
Shrouding precious jewels
In an organic beige muslin—

A charming clandestine dignity.
Note, everyone is beautiful once
In a lifetime, the longevity of this
Beauty is sculpted from earthen clay,
Once white as Adam's rib and as malleable.
She is a day unfolding, with a whispered
daring secret
Too daring, to share aloud, they haunted her,
she cried as quietly as sorrow would allow.
Her face is a chalice, brimming with the salty
life of memory, responsibility, and
unwavering hope.

Mary

The poem "Mary" is partially fictional, somewhat autobiographical, hopefully idyllic and covertly biblical - perhaps. Speaking for myself, I love the subject and progression of this piece. The image of a little girl in her Sunday best, swaying to a melody only she can hear and being the apple of her father's eye, is a daydream I relish. Each stanza is a rite of passage for this young girl, who grows to be an old woman, who simply wants to be a child in her father's eyes again.

Mary

PART I

She was a hesitant daughter.
Demure on a spring day beneath a
Cautious sun and tender, envious
Green sprouts of grass.
I watched her frolic, gallop, and twirl,
The burnished patina of life
Coating the new soles of Easter shoes
Her Sunday best.
Crinoline dusted her awkward knees
While ruffled white stockings cuddled little
feet.
Her dark hair escaped a tidy plait.
Dancing to a timeless melody only she could
hear,
Dizzy with the notes of a solemn waltz.
A smile breaks on the face of her father
Who adores her and
Revels in her innocence and strong will
To simply – just exist in this perfect world.

PART II

She was the belle of the ball

At a traditional cotillion – where rumors
Were sealed and patented on nights like this.
It was a spectacle to treasure and
Recall when memory drifts and fades:
I watched her ebulliently gliding
Across a silky, polished, wood floor – she was
Her father's pride.
Her dark hair swayed and hitched on sweet
tendrils
Framing her lovely face.
Tripping on soft satin toes,
She danced to a song held in her heart.
From as long as she could remember – it was
a melody of
Humble comfort and sumptuous joy.
With timidity demurred, she accepted his
Proffered hand– a dapper suitor, indeed.
With a dainty smile in an effervescent spirit,
They walked – a dance, second to none.
Soon, chirping words tickled her ears
As her court gathered around her,
Fawning and fussing over crowns and
blushing corsages.
This world, this moment, was her bliss.

PART III

She was the embodiment of grace, hope,
beauty, and
Giddy anticipation of the impending rites.
I watched her as a white-gloved hand held
The arm of her father, who, loving her for
years,
Was there to give her hand away.
His pride wrestled with the heartbreak of
letting go.
Walking towards an anxious man, she is
Now held in her husband's rapturous gaze.
She is no longer the girl with awkward knees.
Her dark hair is a halo – veiled
In shimmering seed pearls and old, old lace.
Today folds of satin brush her toes
And she is dancing for all to see.
The beat of her song marking this time and
this place
In her happy heart
Like a precious gem, she is presented to her
father.
They waltz a solemn farewell to tiny dances
On old shoes, in dusky corners --

And all the cherished yesterdays that brought them --
Here, to this joyful moment.

PART IV

She was a solitary figure standing
On the wings of a precious day.
I recall her fondly - the little girl,
The young lady at a cotillion with satin shoes,
and the day she was held close
in her husband's dapper arms.
She had once been her father's daughter
This old woman - I remember her grace
and I surmised she hasn't changed.
Now, her hair was a silver bouffant,
A wren's nest atop a steely head.
It was a chaotic weave of idiosyncrasy,
Time and daily wisdom fraught
With the foam of pain and lessons learned.
She was feeding yellow ducks
In a sudsy green pond – she was
Bent in the form of a crooked letter
With the remnants of yesterday's waltz
snuggled

Contentedly in the tender pleats of her mind
- she sighed.
She simply wished to be his child again.

Soup

Making soup is both a skill and an art. Soup, historically, has had the heavy responsibility of feeding the masses, curing the sick, and comforting the soul. All the while, this simple dish has remained the staunch supporter of the frugal mind. There is a distinct satisfaction experienced in making soup. After a long day with ones and zeros of blue screens, the heft of a knife, the thwack of the cut, and the smell of freshly chopped vegetables is an almost divine experience. If you know, you know. Soup is a staple, soup is an art cultivated by that utilitarian knife and well-used cutting board. This poem serves soup the praise it deserves.

Soup

Elevating the mundane to magnificent
It is an art, making the best of what you have,
The economy of domesticity.
A dash, a dab, a smear, and a smidgen—
The craft of meal preparation.
Leftovers, the Lazarus from the dark, cool tomb,
The Tupperware lidded leftovers, an artist's medium.
The delicate dice,
The cacophonous chop,
The meticulous mince.
The zonal zest of citrus,
The gorgeous grate,
The coy chiffonade,
The patient pestle.
The family caldron, scarred and not too pretty,
It is seasoned with a silky coat, ready to simmer.

The handed-down, cast iron kettle, a Dutch
oven.
Serves without a pretentious attitude.
The resulting creation is wholesome and
worthy,
Of the Le Cordon Bleu, a James Beard, or a
Michelin
A masterpiece!

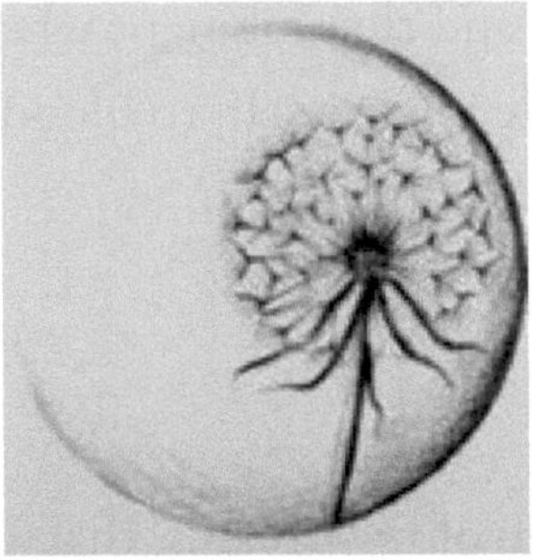

Dandelion

The Dandelion is often considered a nuisance, but I love that happy yellow face and its determination to "go forth and conquer" in any environment. The flower has several incarnations as it sprouts, blooms, and eventually transforms into a white puff of seedlings; they are carried by the wind to their next adventure. A note for the reader, the white thistle is called pappus and can travel over 500 miles. As a child, and admittedly an adult, I would make a wish and blow on the fluffy bristles in hopes my wish would also be carried forth to bloom in another field. This poem uses the life cycle of the Dandelion to illustrate the difficulties of a relationship and that moment when you let go and let life plant itself, to bloom in another field, to live again.

Dandelion

When I let go of my dreams, that
double-fisted cerebral release,
The heavy, sodden, and swollen pieces of my
cardboard heart
Break away and disintegrate in my clumsy
hands.
The carefully and tightly articulated folds
Of recycled experience and new, raw material
Absorbs only so much, and a little more of
me dies.
Like the errant downy thistle of a
summertime dandelion
The pappus becomes a missile in a tempest.
The topsy -turvy somersault of a dream
Is pitched forth from its wellspring of seeds,
And dispersed, lost from view and eventually,
Washed away in the muddy sludge of time.
The sands of an hourglass, soundless in its
narrow passage

Substantiates the misspent hours of a silly
girl.
This paper-doll woman, with her shoddy tabs
and tags and flaps
As delicate as the thistle of a dandelion.

The Beehive

A few years ago, there was a disturbingly large beehive in a tree that arched over the highway. The first time I saw the hive my sunroof was open as I passed under the behemoth – only once though. For the next year, as the seasons passed and I traveled under that hive I watched it shrink, its tattered paper walls fluttering in the wind. It remained in the tree for many months past its lease date; it was a marvel of architecture as it should not have survived the harsher seasons. That beehive was a testament to nature's permanence in a very disposable world and it deserved some humble words on the page.

The Beehive

We all saw it, a dry shroud,
The cinereal hue of a wordless newspaper.
When the leaves turned for the season,
The paper aerial roost above our heads
Caught our attention
And held it.

Only in the previous season,
The architects swarmed and mingled,
Salty nectar of masticated wood.
Paper mâché sculpted into pulpy papyrus
walls
Waiting for the arrival
Of busy bodies with a stinging hello.

The gray husk was slowly unraveled,
A waltz with the wind
The once sophisticated marvel
Of the busy bodies slowly succumbed to
The relentless ribbon of wind and time,
Undoing stitches, undoing seasons, undoing
time.

The eve of the solstice finds
Ebbing, weaving notwithstanding weather
now a bottom-less bleached shroud
Solstice passes, New Year sings
The only mark of time
Was the ragged and frayed edges.

Like the collapsing walls of a footprint
In the sand, a slow and predictable crumble
Ebbing, erasing recent memories,
Time and the experience of rough winds
Fostered decay, the roughly hewn walls
Fell from their perch to be absorbed into the
earth.

Stones and Bones

The neighboring state to Vermont has one of the oldest and largest cemeteries in the area; you cannot miss it. A cemetery is much more than a final resting place. It is a chronicle of lives once lived, a repository of history, a keeper of unsolved mysteries and a silent witness to sorrow and... kinship. Monuments and headstones can mark the time spent on earth, but not the life of the soul below. This poem looks at a cemetery from the point of view of an outsider looking beyond the gates; hopefully it portrays both the luminescent beauty and the ponderous reality of a historic cemetery.

Stones and Bones

Evergreen trees create a revolving
kaleidoscope with the pale sunlight in this
quiet space,
In a defiant and direct contradiction to its
intended purpose, a restful sleep.

The stones, slabs, and mute statutes produce
and sustain life in a mossy cloak
The dead should have a decipherable name, a
written memory – a dash.

The velvet and knitted brocade of verdant
lace of this ancient plant is trying
To erase memories with lichen and evacuated
webs of spiders among the sun's rays.

There is the palpable silence of a thousand
souls left mute in their wooden closets
Well-tended cashmere green grass tells the
story of the absent footprints.

There is only predictable ratcheted clicking of
a hollow-boned tree frog,
And a mourning dove weaving her lament on
the tendrils of a reluctant wind.

Her song in the bashful, blushing evening
tells the power of the word "was"
An unbearable heaviness, a past tense, a
silenced heartbeat.

A shared silent reverence is brought on by an
empty place,
The exquisite weight of a beautiful soul, no
longer enshrined in the flesh.

Headstones and grave ledgers mark time and
guard the flinty path and cornerstones,
They are seemingly contradictory, like
Featherstone, a mason and Priest, a beloved
husband and father.

There are no Papal saints here, there are,
however, the common variety

The mother, the sister, the father and the son;
the good soldier and the desperado and the
lost child.

With quiet auras, these are the sleeping souls -
the secret sinner and the public saint,
A hymn recollecting memories from
experience, the good - the memorable and the
unforgettable.

The wind curls around these monuments, the
fluid dance of unbound souls,
No longer shackled by age on earth, whether
creaking-bone old, or blushing young.

The living observer may suspect, but never
find an answer in the inkwell of memory.

On Being a Poet

Poets are dead white men who used words like, hitherto, ere, alas and thus. The women poets are crazy or ostracized, unique or just existing on the edge of a polite society. I am none-of-the-above; I think and I hope. I am a woman who loves words and enjoys the mental exercise of painting my view of the world with words - allowing the blind to see, perhaps. Maybe I am just vain and want a legacy that is bound in print and maybe one day, carved into stone and becoming a small paragraph in a book that young children are required to read in little desk sets. I am a woman who is willing, at this age and in this time, to share her view of the world; this is. my view of the art that is the written word.

On Being a Poet

Am I? I mean, really?
Some days, words are elusive,
Playing an immature game
Of hide-and-seek among the
Well-wrought Pillars of my mind.

Some days, words are little missiles,
Seeking a Niche for an
Explosive and memorable thought—
A Legacy waiting for the frame
Of a ragged book, full of Spine.

Every day, lithe and elegant phrases
Tumble like a graceful gymnast,
Throwing themselves through hesitant air
And landing on the soft pads
Nimble fingers recording the Art.

I bring things to life, bring life to Things,
Use Capitals like little tiaras, elevating the
common
The Oak leaf is not earthy fibers
Wrought from molecules and complex atoms
It is a swaddling cloth for Chrysalis.

Poetry is not about writing, it's about seeing.
A Poet is, after all, an artist
Who closes her eyes, then creaks open
The doors with the rusty Hinges of a
famished
Mind and uses her pen to write herself.

The poet, in sharing her work,
Is writing herself into the foreground
of a Motion picture, where previously
she blended into the backdrop.
It is uncomfortable, and the light is bright.

Without publication, I am
Walking on water and never tasting the
Salt of failure, a Ballerina on the waves
And an explorer of uncharted frontiers,
Until the Pen is laid aside.

Then the rusty hinges purr—a sign of
Release, and regrettably close.
Written by a neat hand
On a soiled scrap of paper—
A receipt, perhaps, a token of an easier Time.

The Hope Chest

My mom has this beautiful cedar-lined hope chest; as a child, I loved rummaging through it, and having her explain to my young self what each object was. These were artifacts that represented her life; memories that were attached to objects with a rich story held in her heart.

The Hope Chest

Evocation Artifacts
Remember who belongs to you.
Sepia photos muted by the indignity of time,

Instead of the fashionable colloidal sheen.
Dog eared frayed corners upstaged
Only by the oily tarnishing from
fingerprints.
Paper artifacts
Pleased to inform you,
Congratulations,
Happy to announce,
Proud to share with you,
It's with a heavy heart we note...
Textile artifacts
Gossamer veil of confirmation,
White patent of a hard-soled baby shoe,
Beige with age, a lost tooth,
The silky threads of two-colored tassel,
The heavy silk.
Crumbled artifacts
Potpourri of a tissue shrouded first
carnation,
A papery husk of a four-leaf clover, pressed in
wax,
The dried and cracked sequins of a dress,
A child's first foray into pottery, without
purpose.

History is a trousseau –
Love preserved in the cedar notes of memory.

The Second of June

There is nothing particularly deep about this poem. Spending an early morning outside on the second of June my thoughts drifted towards the cherry blossoms in Washington DC. It was a very short connecting flight, in my mind, to the book *Memoirs of a Geisha*; the dedication and effort connected to the attire and makeup of the Geisha is something to behold. I simply drew a parallel between what I was witnessing in nature and the goals of adornment for the Geisha, per the book. The teetering of the Geisha on polished okobo (wooden shoes) and the hesitant entrance of summer is paired together.

The Second of June

A blush on the nape of any otherwise pale
landscape
Of the eastern sky provoked a lusty morning.
The dim obsidian of night faded
And the crisp edges of a porcelain day
hesitantly unfurled.

There was a solitary hot pink petal
On the heirloom crabapple tree,
The fuchsia bloom holding an encore
A final curtsy, a deep bow in the symphony of
spring.

Summer is waiting in the wings, perched on
platforms of memory
While the clouds glided and pirouetted, a
sleek, glossy, silk
Obi tied across the bluebird sky, adorning the
young sun.
Artful, tender shoots weave a flocked-green
tapestry of grass and seed and mirth.

The Course of a Day

Sunflowers rebel against gravity and beauty standards. Standing tall, with a complete disregard for symmetry, their bright yellow petals and encircling hundreds of tightly packed seeds, the sunflower is a force of nature. If you have been fortunate enough to witness the life cycle of these giants, you will recognize the exhausted bowed neck of a sunflower after its glory days appreciating the earth with its sunny, happy face. The weight of its purpose prompts the stem to bend, right below its bloom and droop, as if it already knows its task, here on our fields and yards, has run its course.

The Course of a Day

The melancholy sunflower, too brash for
Its neighbors, the peony and the poppy,
Had hunched its exhausted shoulders
In the misty early morning.
Greeting its beaded brown face is
The earnest sun, cupping the weary petals
And ardently kissed
The heavy neck
With a lover's thirst.
Summer's flower raised its
Fruitful head and held
The gaze of its traveling admirer.
Another day has begun -
The pair beam, rise and fall
Traversing the sky until
Envious evening arrives.
The sunflowers slouches
With a dejected sigh
This day is done.

The 37th Handshake

Recently, I came across an anecdote that I found intriguing: when the Supreme Court justices meet, all nine of them exchange a total of 36 handshakes. The handshake is an ancient tradition, originating as a gesture to show one was unarmed. Over time, it evolved into a common practice in modern society. The premise of this poem is what happens after the obligatory handshake is done, whether you are at a party, a symposium, a new job or with any new group of people, there is that one person you want to come back to. This is the 37th handshake.

The 37th Handshake

The person you came back to --
A second glance, a stutter, a pause.

Human roulette, round and round you go,
Where you land, where YOU land—
Nobody knows. No one knew that day,
That afternoon, that night would cast
The mold of a memory --
An impenetrable cast perhaps
A daydream turned into reality, perhaps –
A lesson that drapes a dark pall
On the timeline of personal history and
memory.

The Circus Comes to Town

Temporarily stepping onto my soapbox here. There is a very slim category of acceptable looks. I cannot speak for the rest of the world, as I only have expertise in my own little niche. There are insiders and outsiders, occasionally there are a few people who are insignificant enough that they can be easily overlooked. The commonality that I wish were more broadcasted is, we are human. We are born the same way, we live, we rejoice, we cry the same salty tears, and we die with the same cessation of breath. Whether we try to stand out or blend in, we are the same.

The Circus Comes to Town

I am the bearded-lady in the circus sideshow,
Howling from behind bars and peddling my
wares.
Fat, disfigured, and deserving
Of the stares that greet my green eyes.
I am nature's creation -
Gone wrong in the narrow prism of society.
I cry myself to sleep
In the manger under the stars
Like a myth, my pillow is straw -
And my future holds no promise.
My dreams come true and false as well.
I see my breath, a dissolving mist,
Like spiders being born -
And my tears are beautiful,
Tiny ice sculptures etching my cheeks.

Hunger

Ah, romance, lust, love, sex, desire – it's the same for everyone; even aspiring poets try to capture the sentiment in wanting someone.

Hunger

I want to crawl into the cloak of the sun
and heal my wounds with fire,
igniting dormant nerves that once craved.
Just now, they are responding to an innate
rapture,
captured in the ghostly recollections of
yesterday.

I want a honeyed balm that leaves raw
emotion
at the threshold of a dusty door

in a cluttered mind --
one that soothes and caresses and inspires
with the lusty tongue of promise and hope.

I want to shed the yellow coat of
disenchantment
and dream vivid dreams where you are
standing in a sea of blushing blooms, where
pockets are holding indulgent hands and
memories as weightless as laughter.

I want you to ask the question
that can only be answered in a pale silky
whisper.
Call me a muse, but when you look at me and
Turn away in a blush, I'm satiated in the
thought – all you gave me
Was the inspiration to write the poem of a
full life.

On Housekeeping

Every person has strengths and areas that could use a little refinement.. I'm decent at school, relatively satisfactory with writing and I possess an unquenchable desire to be better tomorrow than I was yesterday. However, I am not a good housekeeper. In all fairness, how can one be both a meticulous homemaker and a poet? I do see poetry in having a less-than-immaculate house. I see a seahorse in the dust, riding the risers of my staircase like Don Quixote in a field of windmills – charge...

On Housekeeping

There is a clump of ashen dust
On the bottom step
In the shape of a disgruntled seahorse
The amber wood grain
Provides a stoic platform
To be ridden with grace, a knight and his damsel.
The seahorse mounts
And swiftly traverses the ambient air
As exotic feet bound the steps.
Each heavy tread a buoyant surge
Of dancing manes and crescent shoes
At the end the equestrian will rest
In a tidy corner
Exhausted and exulted
The seashore awaits its moldy companion
To be swept away in the romance of a poem.

Autobiography

I am not old enough to write an autobiography, but I can pen a poem about growing up.

Autobiography

I've come into my own lately.
It took me millennia to arrive here – it seems
I know now I am not frivolous...
Well, maybe I am, perhaps - that is not either
here or there...

I am not sarcastic or sardonic,
but I have a funny way
about me and I love to make you smile.
I tried on sincerity once – long ago

and I liked the fit.

My motives are understated, but clearly understood
my dreams are real enough and my pain simply is...
All in all I like what the mirror sees -
Reflected right to left, sole to tarnished tiara.

I'd like to have someone say – You're ironic" --
a portrait of paradoxical wit,
but I don't think they will today.
Looking back I don't think they ever have –
and that's okay too.

I'm whimsical enough to embrace the adage -
I'm not a puzzle to be solved, but a mystery to be lived.
I am geeky enough to know that *geek* is derived from the Dutch
And cool enough to not mention that aloud with new friends.

I am a work in progress, needing primer to smooth the rough edges

Paint, with a deep base, and the occasional
touch-up.
I have not lived enough to be a memory for
the masses.
But, I may be a hint on the edge of the mind,
of something great.

A Man Observed in a Small Country Town

Years ago, I came across a public plea for used suitcases for foster kids. Without a suitcase, kids are shuffled from home to home, bundling their clothes in garbage bags. This fact brought to light the plight of the homeless, whether it is temporary or permanent. This poem sees a man carrying his belongings in a bag, his body weary and his determination apparent. The rhythm of the feet hopefully elicits the mechanical determination to move forward when we do

not necessarily have a destination or a
comfortable place to stay.

A Man Observed in a Small Country Town

Salvation clothes hung on his thin frame -
Yet he walks.
With purpose – with shame
With neglect of the very soul
That drives his weary feet:
Right, left, right,
Right -

Now he is his own.
A hero, a champion – his companion, his own
sadness.
A man walking.
The Story of All,
That we cannot bear to be –
Poverty's bones march with forgotten
memories –

A plastic bag is his humiliating suitcase, his

Secret burden. His pride is sustainable for tonight
Head down, the sun is ashamed
Of his face – Yet
He is a man,
Walking right, left –
Right.

Ballerina Darling

I was living in Burlington in August 1997; I remember every detail of the moment I heard Princess Diana had died. Her death was my generation's JFK's assassination; words could not express the physical feeling of your heart breaking over the death of a stranger. Diana was a princess, a queen with a global impact on all who watched her graceful actions. No one knows what went on in her mind, her daily life under constant scrutiny; but, what we did see was her kindness, her gentleness and her love of mankind – her humanity was a commandment to emulate and follow. This poem was inspired by Diana, whose presence on the stage was beautiful, memorable, and sorrowful.

Ballerina Darling

She takes her position with a melancholy smile
Realizing what she has
And grateful that she was, but she wanted more than this.
Yesterday, she exhaled from a lifetime spent in a corseted role.
And those who heralded her, who followed her with unwavering awe,
Fell silent, mute, dumb-mouthed and struggling to form palatable words.

Dancing as fast as she could
She held her breath, her head high, her crown perched
The applause gave her life, reason,
A stir of oxygen—
Then she exhaled, tipped but barely askew – the applause was paralyzed
As if slapped, a stinging alarm

Wrists down, limp hands,
Covered impromptu jutting knees – they
forgot ceremony for a moment
Gaping in silent despair, outrage, curiosity,
condemnation

Her feet still moving she gained
Her breath – the damage was done
As if behind the wheel into a yawning,
unknown destination,
The leap, the return to earth – absolute, not
forgiving
Forgotten, a dream – an inhalation of hope
With no promise.

Dancing as fast as she can,
She holds her breath, complete cessation—
No longer uncommon
Now uncommonly bold, the attention to a
star ready to fold.
A melancholy smile reflected
In a framed headline:
"Dancer Dies in Auto Crash – World Mourns
Loss of a Rare Beauty."

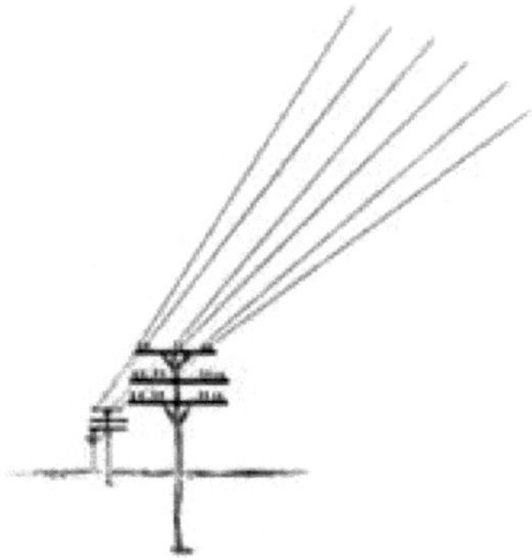

Beside the Highway

I cannot tell you the difference between Monet and Manet, but I know the impression I get from their work – it is a muted world. The pastels illustrate life in a gentle way. Art isn't confined to canvas; it lingers in everyday moments, even in the median of a highway. The grasses, the tossed brown beer bottle and the detritus of a day become faded pastels under the sun of afternoon.

Beside the Highway

Beside the highway, in the median and on the
sloping shoulders,

Lies a gallery of Manet and Monet,
impressions of living.
Dry, mustard-yellow grasses lie dormant,
sleeping sheaths -
Winter is shedding its brittle skin.
There is a dented hubcap lying prostrate
On an abandoned pole, each is splintered and
neglected.
Some wag of a salesman, who passed in a
smudged blur,
Left it standing, forgotten, baring the faded
gray of old metal.
The dirty, barren median, was a decoupage of
refuse,
In stages of fragmenting decay.
Car exhaust creates a blue-grey spume, a toxic
atmosphere.
Grimy fog marred the air and darted -
Beneath the bold bald eye of the midday sun.
The wooden guardrails sagged and looked
guilty -
Shame-faced standing shoulder to shoulder
With technology's new champion.
Metal barriers with mechanical brawn,
Holding ropes and the feeling of security

From unmarked edges and unclaimed graves.
The medium is a diorama of the dash of a life
The sharp, bright start, the dull well-lived
moments,
And the yawning pastels of evening and dusk.

Cassatt's Playground

Mary Cassatt, was an American painter of the late 19th and early 20th century; she is known for everyday moments in family life in a beautiful palette of colors.

Cassatt's Playground

Children play, frolicking in mint-green
dresses,
Inclined askew on tippy toes and bent knees.
With faces of unfiltered, and uninhibited joy
They have blurred little features with soft
smiles,
And a shimmer of innocence –they are

Out-of-doors on a lavender-hued day.
Clouds, like sea-bleached cuttlefish bones,
Play succinct and giddy dances,
Little gigs with flourish on a salmon-colored
morning,
With quiet colors and a pastel lemony sun.
Pale blue musing of those passing-by
Murmur and approve of the sweet antics.
They too recall the muted childhood echoes,
Of a verdant park on a gentle spring day.

9 789369 546855

Printed by Libri Plureos GmbH in Hamburg, Germany